POETRY RISING

Gary N. Miller, Jr. "The G-Mill"

Waid Books

publisher@waidbooks.com

www.waidbooks.com

Contents

Introduction

Like so many others I have walked an imperfect path, but through the art of poetry I was led back to the things that are important to me. Family, Community and Spirituality. This is the trinity of me.

Writing has empowered me and ultimately has become the instrument by which I commune with the Most High.. The words I express are an extension of the spiritual connection I have with the Creator of all things. It is this positive force that teaches me how to live, sacrifice and most importantly, how to love. I love hard!

Through the trials of life, I have learned to change my perception from the subliminal values presented by mass media to something deeper and more mystical. I transformed the nature of my fiery tongue to spit knowledge and uplift my family and community rather than to become a statistic. I rose through poetry and I invite you to walk in my footsteps and view my journey through verse, words and imagery.

Welcome to the trinity.

Poetry Rising

FAMILY

This book of poetry represents the connection of collected feelings that we all share.

We all have love for family. This bond we share cements the rock and dirt that form the earth, and it is the love that flows from the mountain tops like rivers forming seas and oceans.

Yes we are the world...yes we are connected.

I'd like to start this poetic journey by dedicating the first session to my mother, because we are all born through the womb to be here.

I remember writing to her back in the early eighties when I went to college. I remember how much I missed her. I remember the poem and how it made us both feel. It was one of the first poems I ever wrote that moved both of us. Because this is my 1st book I thought, what better way to honor the woman who gave me birth.

I thank the Most High that it was you, Mom. I thank God for you always being there for me.

Poetry Rising

Gary N. Miller Jr. "The G-Mill"

M O M

At times I forget...
who is my best girl
who's loved me endlessly
who brought me into this world

At times I forget and replace you with others
I wine them and dine them, and treat them
like lovers
At times I forget
as the years pass on
they all come and go
as you still stand strong

At times I forget
that it's you that I love
and it's you that I miss
when push comes to shove

At times I forget
all that you've done
and that you may know
that you're still #1

Gary N. Miller Jr. "The G-Mill"

WARNING:

TREE OF LIFE

As you cast your eyes upon this family tree
of life
from the root to stem where branches
separate the light
bearing fruits of wisdom through a
connected trend
stem reppin' now
root reppin' way back then

to the first of the original man
do you really understand why this action
was forbidden?
the mixing of a GOD with a man?
almost complicated plans 'cause the
righteous was overran

but time will have its place
and knowledge was the case as our instincts
became erased
and flesh became the sin
the story of Adam and Eve
this is where it all begins

Let me sum it all up with my views on life and death.

LIFE & DEATH

The Mother, the Father, the Sister, the
Brother
repeat it again, over and over
embrace your family tree
is to die indeed so that you can live forever

Grandfather, Grandmother
and as our bodies get tired
our bodies expire
but the energy continues to proceed
as we become the Chi

this is why we breed
come as I release
Life everlasting wants to re-cast me
'cause in that moment, someone was
conceived
yo tell me what the old man wants
what's He wanna be?
Young again
will he be reborn again?

do you think this sounds insane?
well let me elevate your brains
and I wish not for you to resent
but I was a human being in some type of
experiment

now I'm a human doing 110% percent
to be a spirit having a human experience

this is what I meant when I said up-lift
cause when I raise my tone like this
higher and higher
makes me wanna holler
who's your favorite writer?

who's the town crier?

Allah! Allah! Allah! Allah! Allah! Allah! Allah!
Allah! Allah!
and I said it 9 times, 'cause 9 is the Most
High
it's the ether sign
conditioned for the mind
bound to the body...food for your soul
I guess it depends on who it is you know
I just spoke to a man 9 million years old
and I can only tell you what I was told
If centuries pass by, where the hell they go?

and life goes on for what it's worth
but according to the curse, who was it that
claimed death at birth?
kind of makes you wonder
who really got here first?

we're alive all the time but our dust must
feed the earth
it's a fair trade law of the Universe
call of the truest words

all of us walk these Worlds

and I know I just rocked your World
but all worlds come together in peace
that makes it better
find out we've been hanging 'round forever
cause what goes around comes around
the Darma's in the letter,
however, I need not go no further
as I end this piece in peace and in Love for
one another
I figured it out I finally discovered
that through the Word of my Lord
I have overcome this World

I remember writing the mother poem. I remember how powerful the vibration had to be to get my point across.

I have a vision, or I should say I have an image.

<u>MOTHER</u>

I Am Woman

Mother of the one true savior

I am life through the womb, the creator

I am love for the child

I am the beauty of God that makes men stand proud

I am the first and the last

I am the future and the past

I am the here and the now

The Universe takes a bow 'cause it's my nature to nurture

there's no other

like the Mother

Gary N. Miller Jr. "The G-Mill"

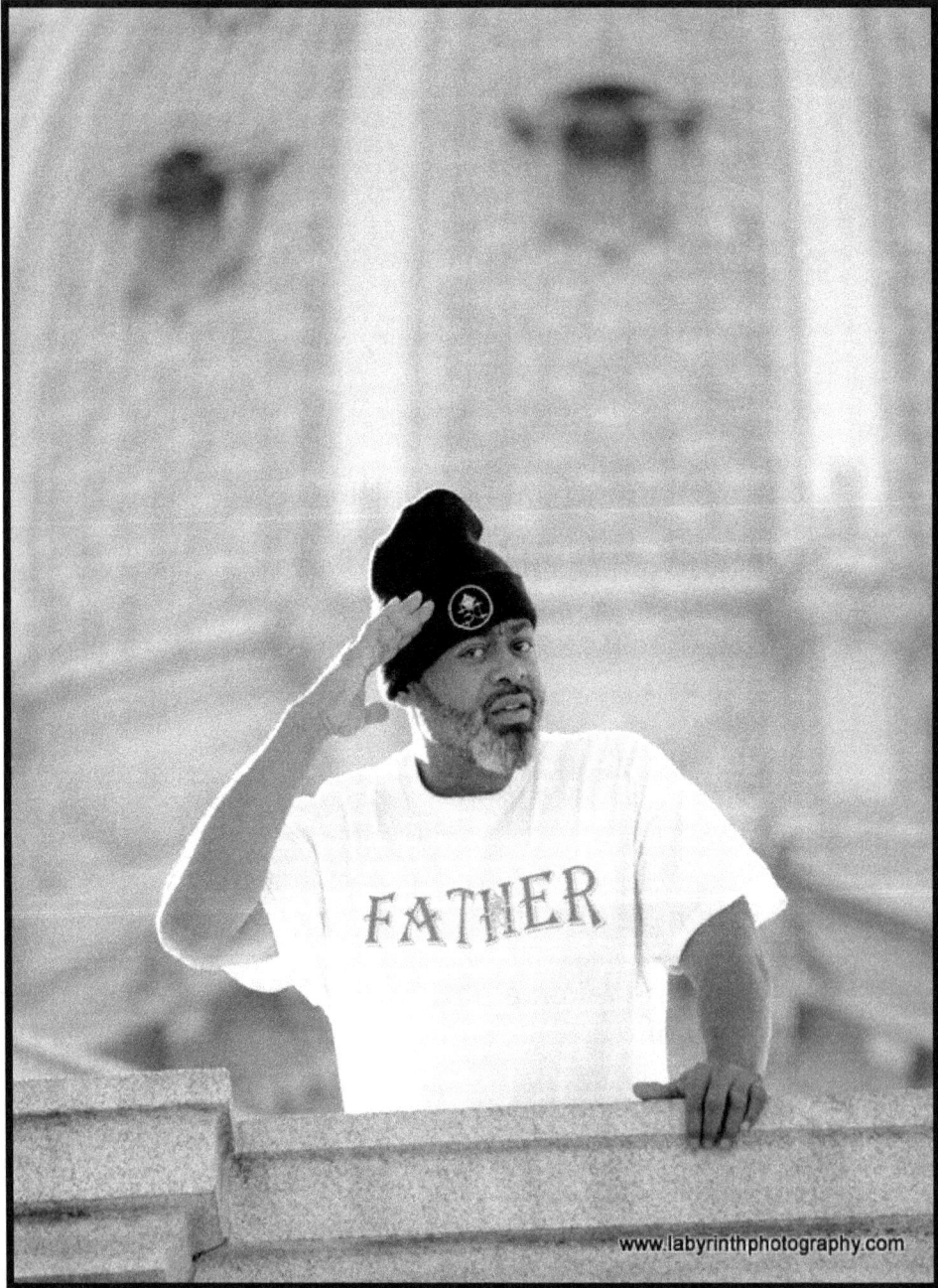

I remember the minutes of one of my first BMD
meetings. BMD - Brothers Making a Difference is a
mentoring program.

My younger cousin always wanted to be the big brother
for the community so he formed his
own organization (BMD).

I remember he said that I should write a poem for each
family member and then we could put the poems on t-
shirts.

I share that vision with my cousin Ellis C. Proctor...they
call him BOOM.

BMD Father Shirt (poem on back of t-shirt)

FATHER

I am like the Father in Heaven

I am like HE, the Creator of Kings & Queens

I am the Father of Dreams

The provider of seeds

Like water I am the Father
That flows when needed
I am like the balance of nature
I am the Father that nurtures so my children
can cater to me
I am like the Father

Every day I Succeed.

Get your BMD Father shirt!

My Father is a serious dude. I honor and respect him.
Love him too.

When I wrote the poem for the Sister it was easy. My oldest sister (Dawn Johnson) and I are so close that our teacher Ahmad used to call me "Dawn Jr.".

She will be put into the book of life for her good deeds.

<u>SISTER</u>

Whether she's older or younger
She's the 9th Wonder
there's no voice stronger

Like the Loudness of Thunder
Or the sound of a sacred whisper
Nothing compares to the Love of a Sister
Uplift her with the things she needs
God bless her for her deeds

Please stand & deliver
Clap your hands for the winner
Keep her days full of joy
Much deserved for my Sister

Maia is my younger sister we are connected in more ways than one she is so talented. She will have everything to do with things to come, she is that grounded, yes I claim that.

Back in the day I was a BIG fan of Public-Enemy. So when I met Professor Griff and presented him with a BMD Brother t-shirt, I felt like one of the SW1's. This poem reminds me of that day.

<u>BROTHER</u>

Peace be unto you my Brother

May your final hours be blessed with God power

Let the sour taste of struggle and trouble

Be smothered with love and respect for one another

Let the will of our minds

If just for one time

Combine in the spirit of crimson, ebony and clover

'Cause it's never over 'til the truth is uncovered

So peace be unto you my Brother

I'd like to dedicate this poem to the one who knows me best. She recites my poetry better than me sometimes. She listens and hangs on my every word. She is my confidant, is always by my side and my roommate.

She is my best friend and I Love her

<u>LOVE OF A BEST FRIEND</u>

A friend, a smile, a pleasant comment
A time in mind we'll share
Like the seasons rotated by the spinning of
the Earth
Like a child of Love when she entered this
World
Like the first time we met

A beginning or birth

I'll cherish our ways of conversation
like playtime at recess

and even though I'll never possess you
like I would a bouquet of flowers
placing you in the solar light
quenching your thirst for laughter
hearing the tone of your voice vibrating in
the space that I occupy

I'll admire the scenery from across the
rooms that we both balance
Breathing the same air

Loving the way you are

www.labyrinthphotography.com

COMMUNITY

As I venture into the topic of community, I get an unsettling feeling due to the lack of unity and leadership. It is here where I crossed paths with the organization BMD (Brothers Making a Difference), formed to counteract the negative mindset of our neighborhoods.

BMD has given me the opportunity to work directly with the youth, allowing the seeds of positive thought to be planted through poetry. The organization was formed by Ellis Proctor and because we share this vision of a greater nation we will always be connected. I thank the Most High for restoring purpose in my life through BMD, through Ellis (Boomer) Proctor and for the timing of it all.

Poetry Rising

THE FACE OFF

this poem is a familiar story

a little bit like my story

bits of fame - sometimes pain, but I know
it's all good for me

kept me sharp

even though I still worry about my heart

because when it comes to me I'll trust
almost anybody

but when your partner is that somebody and
you don't wanna break-up

and you don't wanna be locked up and you
don't wanna get boxed up

so I guess it's time to pack up 'cause the
children wanna act up

here's a fact

detach

do I even want this back?

...THIS is how I react...

and it hurts with all its might

but safety is the foresight

and-that makes it all right

all night and all day

any way you cut it got to take the time to
pray

so I took the time to say

God give me strength

Ahumdul-Allah

now I'm no longer afraid

watching life unfold, embracing the change

and I'm gonna need some change

'cause this money thang always got me
needing thangs

am I really running thangs?

this can be so punishing but I know I'm
running things

pushing for perfection, learning all my
lessons

but deception put me in the wrong direction

the truth came out

here comes the blessings, the things that
I'm expecting

all my dreams

thoughts of a King

every time I come in here you know I cause
a scene

'cause I'm settin' them free

'cause your story is my story especially
when I speak in terms of we

'cause the world is in me, like the world is in
you

and a man's got to do, what a man's got to
do

momma always said son, don't be no old
fool

now I'm cooking with soul food

what your momma said

"man that's old school"

now go tell them what I told you

see, life includes them all

all the good and all the bad

did you know the balance of happy - sad?

and if I cry now, later then I'll laugh

one thing's for sure

this too will pass

right out my ass 'cause the shit that's coming out of me

must really bother me

never expected to be crying in my poetry

but I'm letting you in so you know of me

and I'm pulling down the fence but it's getting just a bit intense

'cause I'm taking a big risk

but it makes a lot of sense

The G-Mill has a weakness

'cause I'm a pillar of strength

and I know the death of times brings life

so take a pinch, more than an inch

make sure it's a whole bunch 'cause these
moments get rough and if I were you

I'd bring a lunch

when I get this feeling

call it a hunch

trouble comes in doubles and it can bury you
like cement rubble

but I rise top side like champagne bubbles

'cause I'm on this God level and I went
directly to satan the devil

and I said "listen man, you've got to leave
me alone, I'm not standing on my own. I'm
under the instruction of Yahweh El-Elyon!"

And he goes, "oh my bad, but you know I
like to roam.

Think you'd better make that known. So
take your cry-baby ass on home! By the way
G-Mill, you'll do ok. You may not pass all
your tests but he knows you'll do your best."

and Then I said, "what makes you think I'd listen to you?"

and He goes "well the one that you call father, he's my father too."

and I said "damn, what an awesome thing to say. I'll be going on my way, you go and do what you do and have the damned day."

Minutes later I was at my doorway

Momma plant one on me now 'cause your daddy's home to stay

***alt ending (but I won't ignore the signs, sorry Daddy can't stay)

Let me **REMOVE THE DOUBT**

The letters come in the mail to plant the
seed of doubt
I, like the rain, came to wash the lies out
I, like the Son, came to retrain all your
brains
say "this is what I do this is what I bring"
 and my guitar don't need no strings

supersonic waves when I do think
heat from the vibe makes it 3-D
I'm dimensional - It's intentional
and I'll take this flow to da heartbeat
subliminal when I do teach
penetrate your domes to the white meat

I just wanna be free, that's just like me
and I'll take you to church when I do speak
truth's gonna hurt someone's feelings
best come correct with your dealings
wanna start healing try to start listening

try to reconnect with your instinct
what this is for real is a G-Mill sighting
light from the eye
check my high beam
fire from the sky check the timing
microphone check
do you hear your ears ring?

well answer me

is the poetry appealing?

then praise all of his names when your
kneeling
and pray every day cause you're willing
I just wanna pray till it tears through the
ceiling

cause this IS love that you're feeling

<u>and</u> I just saved 40 billion
the people wanna know from Tibet to New
England
that YOU are the rhyme to the reason
and YOU have control of your season
let the MOST HIGH be your guide
let all parties subside
yes that's pleasing
I think I said enough so I'm leaving
don't wanna over stuff when I feed them
lead them like the Medium
I believe I removed all doubt
...The G-Mill's out

When I raise my tone like this I say: REAL MEN DON'T QUIT

REAL MEN DON'T QUIT

Men, it's time to be men again can you
remember
so open up your hearts and let the kingdom
in ya
and as your King I'll serve ya
put newness back into ya
so that you can remember that you were
once the ruler
now return this to the sender and I'll stand
up as your mentor

the last air bender just broke the sound
barrier
with truth and facts I'll bury ya
but your righteous acts will carry ya
from out the grave America

cause them other guys still fearing ya
but you know that I'll speak clear to ya
so you can be familiar
with this energy I'm feeling ya

God knows that we're superior
now look at all my warriors

I said look at all my warriors

and then look at all my warriors

now look upon each other,
and recognize your brother
the God inside's forever
this flesh is just a cover

so don't be no jealous fellow
and don't be no God killer
cause we all got God in us

I just served you God's dinner

and you know his word will fill us
and what I feel it's the realest
unsealed G-Mill top thriller
Top Ramen chicken flavored

and if I told you that I'd save you from the
haters
then you'd better love it now...not later
and now you know that I cater to the all
mighty style of Allah the Creator
and-for the rest of my life I'll remember his
plan for me
my God
man he made ya
is it up to me to change ya?
try a different story, break down your
shameful glory
barking like dogs ain't for me,
thinking like a canine wanna do you all the

time
low-level reptile minds

take it as a sign cause I don't want no one
to fall
this could be your wake-up call

man, this is for us all
you can have whatever you want
according to the Universal Law
this lesson's raw
hard core
time to be a man and stop acting like the
beast ridden whore
that ain't what you came here for

nothing should deter you from before
stay focused just a little more

cause that's the same ole door
and if your tired of taking less
well let me give you more of this spoken gift
POWER gushing out my mouth
full throttle
cause I split my lip and as the blood starts
to drip
I think I speak for us all when I say that
"Real men don't quit!"

Gary N. Miller Jr. "The G-Mill"

I speak to the young man as well....

THE G-MILL MAKES A DIFFERENCE

OOOOooooo
"SMOKE" from the dragon's lair...
To the young minds of seemingly desperate
times
death dealers and senseless killers...haters
of their own kind
some of this is going to rhyme
so I'll pray on a rhythm

'cause I want you to claim this vision

you know we all gotta die
but how you die makes a difference
doing the right thing can insure your
existence

so for those of you with even smaller
children
TEACH them
but you don't know

so let me TEACH YOU about this flow
about this moment about this inner glow
restore what was stolen
the FUTURE is what you're holding

and as for me I've been chosen
to re-open the unjust case files
from the African X files and this thing goes

on for miles
but you know that I'm coming
wisdom words got the winds-a-humming
hope you're listening mouth still running
now I'll summing artifacts
when you read this it makes you say
that's the Power of Persuasion

as I attach into your intellect
"aint that amazing?"

no need to tap into facts
but the fact is we need praising
Love, Respect and Peace...Bring It Back
this is what I'm craving
this is where it's at
if you're gonna die...make sure you dye it
Black...
so let your death make sense
die to the negative and become someone
making a difference

Peace to the young peeps.

I call on all of the modern-day disciples

TONGUES OF FLAME

Tongues of flame, sons of light
let us come together in a circle where we
chain it tight
and as Kings of the ring we unite
become stars of the night
of the sound table I invite
pictured words worth 1000 gigabytes
as the fire ignites
let it burn
it'll change your life

and you know I speak it right
yeah this is how I write this is what you get
when i recite
heated smoke chokes me in my wind pipe
but I gotta let it out cause my larynx is way
too tight
blazing mics with my mouth
I said stop drop and roll
'cause I'm hot just like the south
you can really feel me when I make it loud
goose bumps and wisdom lumps assist me
as I move the crowd

and I'm Black and I'm Proud
that's an old rule from a bold crew

and I'm sold at the fact when I got back I

chose you
and I don't know if you're ready for the
whole truth
but what we need to produce is knowledge
for the new school
so these young dudes can come up off these
bad moods
if we gonna make it through make your beds
so you can choose
'cause it's time to make moves

RED ALERT if your children's out there acting
like fools
RED ALERT if you think your woman's being
untrue
RED ALERT if you see a pimp in a red suit
RED ALERT if you think the mirror's looking
at you
'cause that's not your reflection
you're the image of the creator himself
so stop guessing
start addressing
you don't need no more proof

you're the Gods that they're praying to
I dare anyone to top that news
tongues of flame with a hint of blue
The G-Mill brings it to ya
'cause The G-Mill still rules

*I remember the feeling I had when I heard the
Zimmerman verdict. It was another one of those,
"nothing will ever be the same" moments. Sad and
outraged at the fact that we've seen this before. What to
do but to write the truth? I wrote it as if someone else
was in the room guiding my lines. I remember the peace
I felt after the passionate encounter I had with the inner
energy as it poured out of my thoughts onto the paper.*

*Now connected to your own opinions I remember the
familiar shock of the past and the pain felt across all of
the urban communities in this Nation. This is what I
wrote…*

BLACK LIFE/VENGEANCE IS MINE

VENGEANCE is mine
sayeth he who dwells in I
you cannot trust a liar once they told the
great lie
A Masonic secret to promote genocide
Watch close as your bloodline is being wiped
aside

VENGEANCE is mine
a message for the deceased if you lay with
the beast
you will be slain with the beast
for those who gave power to the UNITED

SLAVE system
"Beware"
'cause you just signed a contract to die with
them

VENGEANCE is mine
for those who crossed over
your hated reflection
unwilling to stay sober you despise your own
kind
'cause you choose to stay blind
your death will be rewarded
once I free your boxed minds

VENGEANCE is mine
for those who have lost their way
a man must be a man 24hours a day
when changing his world he must know what
to say
to bring life to his word he must love what
was said
then pray on his knees
to come back from the dead

VENGEANCE is mine
sayeth He who dwells in me
your 'crime'?
the misused knowledge of my family tree
a sacrificed Prince is too much blood to rinse
with words you'll be completely
wiped
from existence

VENGEANCE is mine

with the sword in hand
I remembered murdered cultures, I
remember stolen lands
during the days of your time your actions
were foul
there's no place for you here
BE GONE as of right now!!!

(*Inspired by the MOST HIGH*)

MESSAGE FROM THE VERDICT

The issue is and has always been about

Black Life

the war on Black People has been in effect since

the beginning of American His-story X

the overwhelming hate from our most bitter opponent will never stop

unless we unite as a people

Black People uniting

the thought alone raises fear and should raise the question

why are you so hell bent on keeping us divided?

how can you participate to hate your GOD so much as to bind him

from recognizing his true purpose on this earth?

The Zimmerman verdict is a blatant display of prejudice

reminding us of how worthless Black Life is
in America

I am not a prejudiced man

however

our story tells us that this relentless
disrespect

will continue until we are extinct

it will never change there will never be
peace

unless we unite

NOT Guilty means more to come

so prepare yourselves for the slaughter

so for those of you who kill your own

how dare you raise a gun to your own
image?

your own kind which is that of the Son?

you are committing mutiny in the eyes of

the MOST HIGH

lay down your weapons against each other

respect each other

respect yourselves

if we make peace with each other ALL will be
at peace with us

keeping it 100

I once heard a man say

"NIGGERS are Afraid of Revolution"

I refuse to believe that

LIKE TO UNITE

The Power of Forgiveness

I FORGIVE YOU

I forgive you 'cause when you lie to me
you kill the part where I believed in the
union of
awareness
shared in your company

knowing you would bring deceit
so sad to see you play the role on the dark
side of duality
naughty gin, agent of my enemy
systematically insulting the intelligence
that's not for free
this all comes with a price
past the boundaries of money
this energy can claim your life

so to the drama kings and drama queens
how long will you be willing to set the days
of karma free?
now I'm asking the MOST HIGH to pardon
me

yes
I forgive you
especially for me

When I think about my baby-girls, I just know that they were Heaven sent.

I wrote a poem for all the baby-girls

<u>BABY GIRLS</u>

Why should I worry about becoming a young
lady?
Will someone need to save me?
Won't maturing help raise me?
Is my transformation that devastating?
Will I be preyed upon, hated on, and
sexually gazed upon daily?
Will I be respected by my friends? Or does
that come rarely?
Yet I'm barely old enough to over-stand.
why so scary?

What's out there?

Why must I beware?

Why must I struggle with negative energy?
My enemy?
Watching the world from my room with a
stare
just because I care
I think I'll change it, make the people aware

Help the people get there
So the people can stop looking through the
peep-hole
It's a world out here
Open doors
Open opportunities

So "Open Sesame"
'Cause it's getting sort of strange and this
life is all new to me
So I'll have to stay true to me
'Cause I want to feel safe in the company of
positive energy and this I believe

There's no Love like the Love that I feel for
my mommy
'Cause she stayed up on me
That I may dance on the doorstep of the
One and Only

So you know what I see when the mirror
looks back

THERE STANDS A YOUNG QUEEN

I have some great dreams
I, like the sun, will arrive on the scene and I
said some great things

Moving thoughts with the flow of my art
A blooming seed
Now there's just one more thing and it's my
favorite part

THANK YOU GOD for choosing me

<u>THIS HOUSE IS CLEAN</u>

This is for the audience

I'm all in this, it all makes sense

you're interested in learning this

I'll serve you this, a spoken gift

so concentrate and re-focus your attitudes

the way you cuss

you speak poison to all of us

your mouths I'll curse, your thoughts impure

your heart, I hope's not beyond cure

I do this for the helplessness

my only chance for happiness

I'm Heaven sent, from Heaven's bliss

my spoken word, the angels miss

Gary N. Miller Jr. "The G-Mill"

(singing) [missing one angel child cause you're here with me right now]

and for those of you that don't know of me

I just stopped by to drop off some poetry

don't you know all of this, it was meant to be?

don't you know that my style is all you need?

I'm awareness followed by your energy

and I magically drop it with authority

and I know my life will flow through me

speak in truth and you can rule the galaxies

ain't you proud of me?

you can count on me

I can take you past the point of sanity, but this ain't vanity or debauchery

'cause I'm here by the will of the majority

this is all for free or it ought to be

but it's time you and I got

beyond belief

what's your motive?

know your purpose

are you trust worthy or are ya just thirsty?

drink the spring of living water and get
healthy

'cause I'm your pharmacy

check my frequency, like the perfect
conductor for electricity

I'm the one you see

it's my telepathy

that satisfies all the needs in the place of
peace

put my thumbprint on my dialogue for
identity

don't I do that deed?

don't get strange on me

ain't you tired of that "monkey mind" mentality?

negativity is your only enemy

so stay positive if you want to live

if you wanna receive than you got to give

and this is how I give 'cause this is all there is

this is The G-Mill signing off

trying to stay tuned in

so wont you come on in?

now let's say A-men (pause)

now when I say A-men that's means "be it so"

that's the only way to go

so be it

so speak it

so when I try to get to know you let me in

so I can seed it

and I know it sounds conceited but I am the
center

this is my journey, this is my own personal
adventure

and as I picture my life in the oneness of the
3rd sight

like a bulb light, now the room's bright

cause it sounds right and it's Christ-like

and I should have said it twice with two eyes
full of tears

'cause I'm finally standing here after 2000
years

and what you're about to hear is gonna
sound crystal clear

but fear not what already has been done

because there's nothing new under the

power of the mighty sun

and as my Father, he dances on my tongue

I said my father, Allah, dances on my tongue

because I come, loving everyone

loving everything

this is what I do

listen to your King and what He's telling you

when He's telling you

why He's telling you

every time I drop a line I'm gonna say to you

just before I hit the door and blow this awesome scene

someone say A-men

(*crowd response*)

"this house is clean"

Gary N. Miller Jr. "The G-Mill"

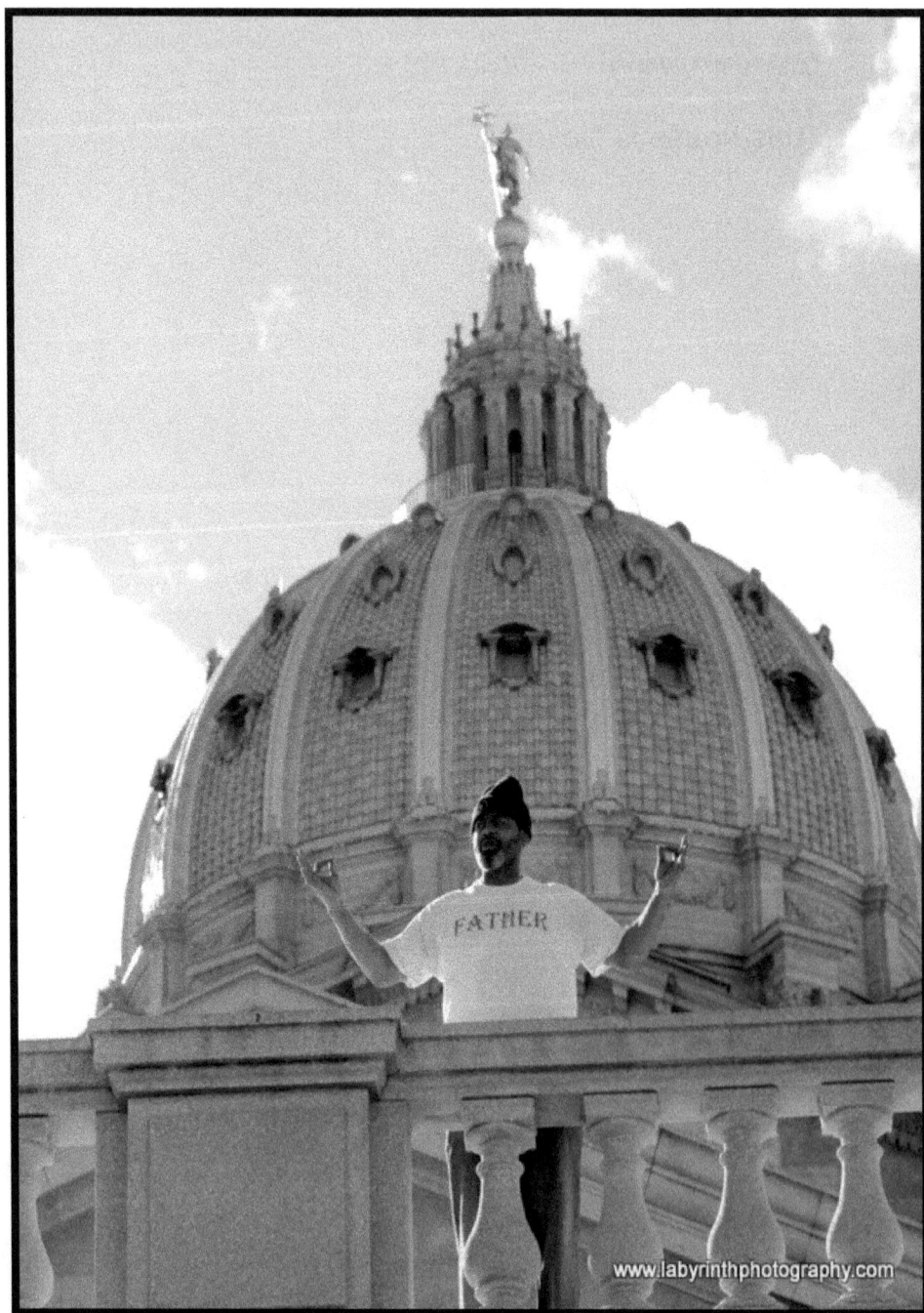

*The family unit is the center of the Universe and because
we all belong to a unit we are all connected*

Let me express The G-Files...

THE PLEDGE

I Pledge Allegiance to UNITE
All of my Brothers, men of color, men of
might
All of my sisters, who believe in what's right
All who listen for the mission to strike
All about the pride
Black Power Rise
All of my people I see you can't hide
All who roll with the "soul-up" side
All for the ones who gave their lives
Anti-Genocide
better recognize
All for the ones who stand in line
All for the prize
battle for the mind
All of my decisions will be
authorized
signed and sealed
by the finger of GOD

Gary N. Miller Jr. "The G-Mill"

All of the times, hate crimes, who's dying?
All of the families destroyed, who's crying?
All about the justice ignored
Who is lying?
All about the rage so I keep trying
All of the world won't be invited

this is how it is
pledge to be UNITED

SPIRITUALITY

Although family and community are as one, the foundation and purpose of life, spirituality, is the strongest of bonds amongst the three. For it includes the energy of the unseen power summoned through faith.

It is through spirit that I have learned how to channel my energy into community and family. My faith was restored through positive instruction from many spiritual teachers and guides. With that instruction I was able to recreate and manifest into my life something greater than just me that was here before me!

I am spirit. I am Poetry Rising.

Gary N. Miller Jr. "The G-Mill"

*I remember a session I had with my son, Gary N. Miller,
III. I call him G. Milll (with 3 L's).*

*He likes to lay back and I say to him, "Train that
body...you have a remarkable build...in fact, train my
body!"*

*I reminded him of my good ole days, and tell him how
much I used to train.*

*When I think of that conversation it reminds me of a
poem...I AM*

<u>I AM</u>

I am not speaking directly to you
but through you
into you
so try not to get confused and as I reach
each
individual
I'm-a try and do my best, so that you catch
this visual
or until you perceive to see past your
reflection
so you understand what you received

and I'm not trying to bring you down but
you're earth-bound clowns gettin' tossed
around
in the lost and found
I am deep in my sound
I am deep in your skin

matter fact I'm past the skeleton
because like you I am
A temporary guest
but I teach with force
not to the flesh
but I with a voice
am like the burning forest
Evolution in progress
now process what I said

I am read
not like the color but like the book...
so look inside
'cause I took the time to combine all our
minds
all at once
always in the Omni-ous
and it's obvious that I pray for all of us,
and all of those that I touch in tongue
I am like the tommy-gun
ah-ah-ah-ah-ah-ah-ah-ah
ah-ah-ah-ah-ah-ah-ah-ah
spit on everyone

Fire from the Son
excessive heat seeping through my teeth
so let the dragon speak
I, like Ramadan, am the chosen one
and I know that we've only just begun to
over-come
with unshakeable faith
meaning E-mon,....sounds like A-mon
that's a-maze-on

'cause I can go on and on
'cause I am spawned from past kings and
future things
I am aware of the present and the gift it
brings
so what I bring as I am writing
is the icing that makes life seem
like bright beams of light
cause I dream

then I scream...whooooo

we all scream for ice-cream
and if you know that phrase you can be on
my team
because my team is mighty
words that invite thee
words that cut like swords of steel

learn to be
still
and focus on what it is that you Will
is what will happen

let The G-Mill teach you how to tap in
I'm your captain
everlasting
always acting in your best interest
I invest, my spirit's in this
and I charge you all to be a witness to the
sounds I shift
my style up-lifts

so take a swing and get a hit

because my intentions are perfect
but there are no perfect men
because like you
I wanna win

so make sure you tell all your friends
that in order to be free

the I must change the I to we

cause you complete me
when I am speaking to the energy inside of
you
I am the elephant in the room
truth be told...

I AM YOU

www.labyrinthphotography.com

Gary N. Miller Jr. "The G-Mill"

I love, live and let live JUST BECAUSE.....

JUST BECAUSE

Just before I sit down to write
Just before I get my head tight
black words to the page white
Just before I make it sound right or make it
sound like
something sacred for your foresight

Just before I start my night, I start my life
Bis me Allah ignites the power of the white
light
Just before I get you hyped
Just before the spiritual war
before you die because you Just
might...mmm...

Just before I talk that talk
I'll walk that walk and never sulk cause deep
inside
I fight the good fight
Just before my mind takes flight or just
before I recite
vibes from the se-kum that's the force from
deep inside

Just because my level's on 9
9 to the most high
Just because Yashua-Bin-Joseph is right on
time

Just because I like to rhyme
that rhythm dance the sadhu chant
and still to this day it's still for man
so let's rewind

Just before you broke that holy bind or
just because the pathway of my spine was
alluded with lies
illusions of death

Just because the 3rd eye on my head was
said to be temporarily
blind

Just before I saw the signs
Just before the energy of djed rose up
through my Chakra line
Just because I say it's all mine
because it is
that's how it is

Just because I got so much love to give
and I wanna shine
Just like the stars in the sky
Just before the door came open and I got
my prize

Just because I finally realized the way it was
the reasons I'm here
to serve my creator

JUST BECAUSE mmm...

(Master: My Son, we are already sons of the Most High)

So let's get focused and...

START WALKING

I GET IT!!!
and get that you don't get it

it's just that wickedness won't release those
who practice it
so don't act as if you didn't get the facts I
left
I'm trying to keep you active
from a lesson in Ecclesiastes
but you laughed at this

the seed that I've sown
unaware that you serve foreigners in a land
that's not your own

and this baffles me
this style that you've condoned
it's like you'd rather eat scraps like a DOG
for a bone!

I shouldn't have said that
forgive me for my tone
forgive me I'm unjust, I'm a sinner, I
confess
but you must admit this world is a mess

but the Lord gave his word that you and I

are Gods at best

little "g"
little gods nonetheless
but a God is a God and that's my inheritance

and as for you it's for all of you as well
it's for you to take this all in...but it's for me
to tell the tale

and I do it well through the training and the
prayer
never mind that I might fail because success
is in the details
so do tell
I'm not selling you religion
I'm just trying to cast a vision
quit my job
live off my spiritual pension

and if you caught that that lets me know
you're listening
and that makes you feel good whether you a
Muslim, or Christian, or a Haitian, or an
Asian, or a Patient
Bismeillaahir Rahmaaneir Raheim
that sound right there
that's ANCIENT!!!

and that's Awesome that I even thought of
you enough to send vibes to your heart
and restart this brand new righteous nation
but it feels like I'm facing this alone

but I got to stand strong
'cause I know where I belong
in the long and secure arms of the Lord
so take part of this walk and the fruits of my
words

Gary N. Miller Jr. "The G-Mill"

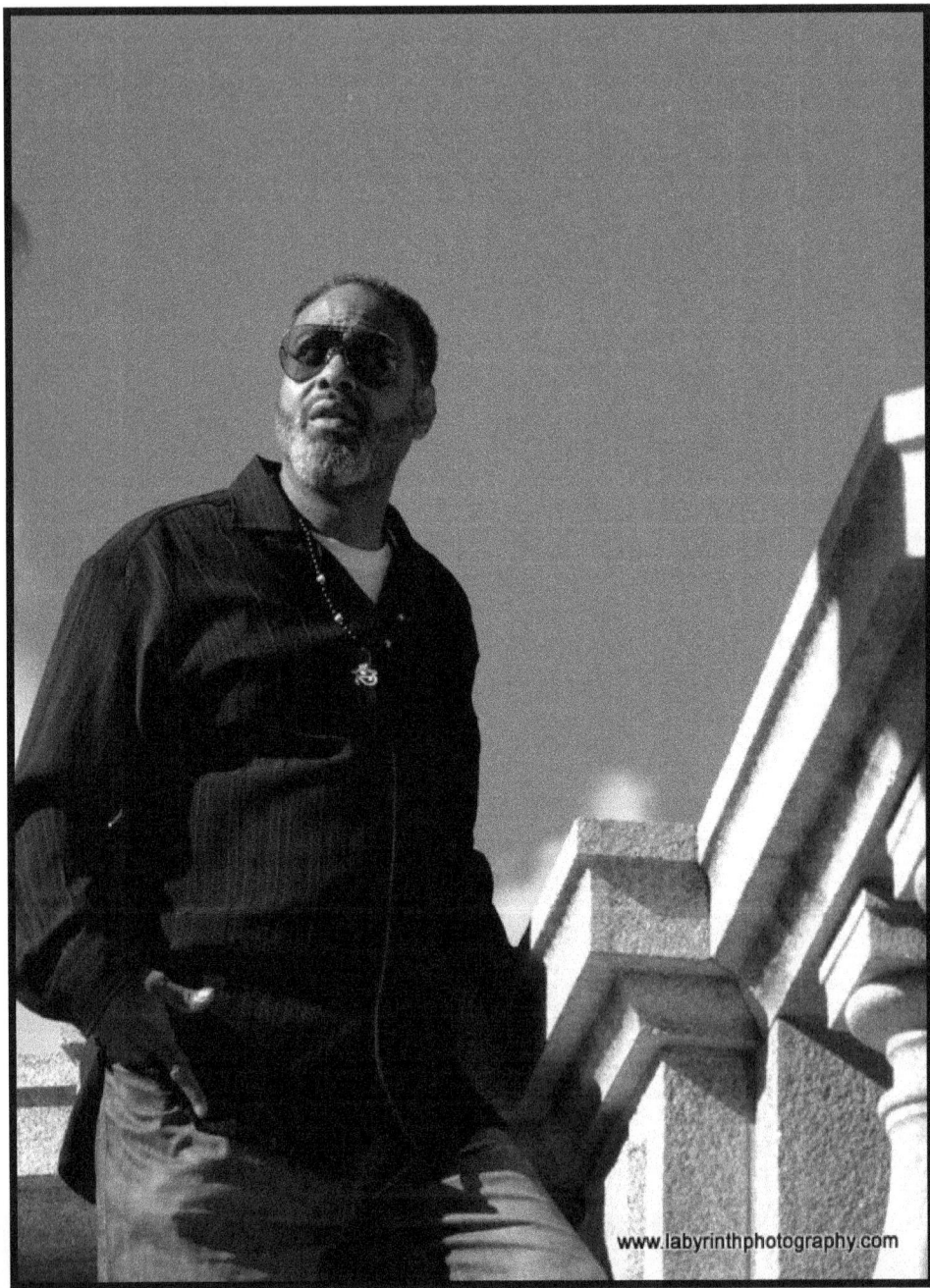

Stay focused!! We must act there is no better time than the present.

Put your energy into what you do best.

TONIGHT

In walks the Lion
you know I'm not lying
iron sharpens iron
listen while I harden your spirit muscles
I'll get you ripped
as I rip holy scripture from my bottom lip

it's a gift so I'll paint a picture til it hits ya
tonight
try and keep your heads out the ghetto
tonight
cause I'mma turn some zeros into heroes
tonight

I'm saying that he rose and that she rose
from the dead
'cause I'm yanking pillows from the sleepy
heads
tonight I'm in the red - hot is my zone
it's a love jones as I bless you with the G-
tone tonight
when you're alone
thank him for the air in your lungs

deep breath
now let it go

tonight
wiggle them toes
meditate on the rate
of the pace that the blood flows
inhale through the nose

tonight your light's gonna shine like a lit
candle glows
tonight everything goes
but tonight is the night
I remind you to be thankful
so I thank him for another day
I thank him for the sound of sermon
and-what it is that I have to say
I thank him for the uncertainty of life
and then I pray
And then I thank him for showing me the
right way
I thank him for the seconds
I thank you for thoughts projected
I thank you for the Word and the way you
left it

I thank you for your methods
The perfect design from spine to mind
I thank you for being here at this point and
time
I thank him for a peace of mind and all that
we'll get
I thank him for the part where I get to say
Hotep
and how it effects the vibrations of the
atmosphere

but don't you fear Hotep means peace
just wanna make you aware
I thank you because you care about where
you're at and where you're going

I'm not lying man
these are the facts
so learn the word
cause this time next month you might not
make it back
so let's just thank him for time spent
and let that be that
tonight

I'd like to keep this flow going with

<u>TRUE PRAYER</u>

BEHOLD!!!
by the power ~~invested~~ in me
through my YIREH the redeemer
by the word we are set FREE
Free from whatever is making life
unpleasant
what's blocking your blessing or what lie
keeps you guessing

and why'd we mess around acting like
beasts
when at the end of the day
there'll be weeping and gnashing of teeth
and the grief
GOD-damn all the wicked
it's a ticket to the Kingdom if you listen to
the message

there is mercy like you wouldn't believe and
the grace starts the day you
repent
on your hands and knees
Father please, cause I'm talking about ME

I'm not judging for no justice 'cause I'm not
always righteous

but I'll say this as I stand before my KING

you can always count on me
sin or saint
to do the right thing
that's my thing, represent the son of man

Be a leader for all men let your light shine
for mankind
get in line cause it's time for your services
our Lord suffered just to serve us
and die as ransom for the masses
meaning many cause the spirit's good and
plenty

when I let the Lord lead it's like 20 out of 20
milk and honey that's the only land for me
YAHWEH keep me
'cause I'm seeking my divine
destiny

and let it start through the praise that I
preach
HOLY, HOLY, HOLY
is the lord GOD Almighty

RETURN TO THE SPIRIT OF ONE

I wanna return to the spirit of one

I wanna feel God

I wanna be sure

I wanna know if you heard this before but I don't wanna lose you

'cause there's a bit more

I wanna take to create a new style to communicate

and I want your respect for your own damned sake

I wanna shout out with just a little faith

"What's up King? What's up Queen? What's good my beloved?"

Life naaameen?

When I dream, I dream of pastures money green

I'm down by the sea sipping on some
ginseng tea

I wanna teach thoughts of Heaven to my
seeds

so tell me what you need and tell me why
you grieve

I wanna show the Lord the lighter side of me

trying to flee from satan 'cause he's hating
on the 3rd degree

I'm mad 'cause he's always on my property

he keeps it rough by touching me

demons get a hold of me

dammit wont they let me be

only god can set me free

sinning in the city that I live in

Jesus be my friend to the end and provide
me with your energy

so when I crush, I crush the bones of my

enemy

give me strength to reign

I'm insane for my family

can you handle me?

down for the cause 'cause when I roll with
Allah

I'm the Dali-Lama

holler at me like your pappy

happy with this poetry

serving up some blessings and love lessons
in the recipe and I'm guessing that you can't
get enough of me

dazed and confused

that's the Lord speaking directly and he's
using me

thank you God for choosing me

what you get is who you see

what I give is what you need

Pleading to my people

take heed

stop the villains from senseless killings and
learn how to disagree

'cause He's coming through the drumming of
the thunder

He's gonna take you under 'cause your sins
cause his wounds to bleed

glad it ain't me

'cause I'm not the saint you see

you all call me The G-Mill but I'm still waiting patiently

to return to the spirit of one

'cause I wanna feel God and I wanna be sure

I wanna know if you heard this before

I don't wanna lose you 'cause there's still a bit more

close doors they seem to get the best of me

does the Lord think less of me?

who you calling refugee?

apologies don't amount to the things that be

so I say this eagerly

pay your dues

follow me

to return to the spirit of one

so that you can feel God

and that you can be sure

Gary N. Miller Jr. "The G-Mill"

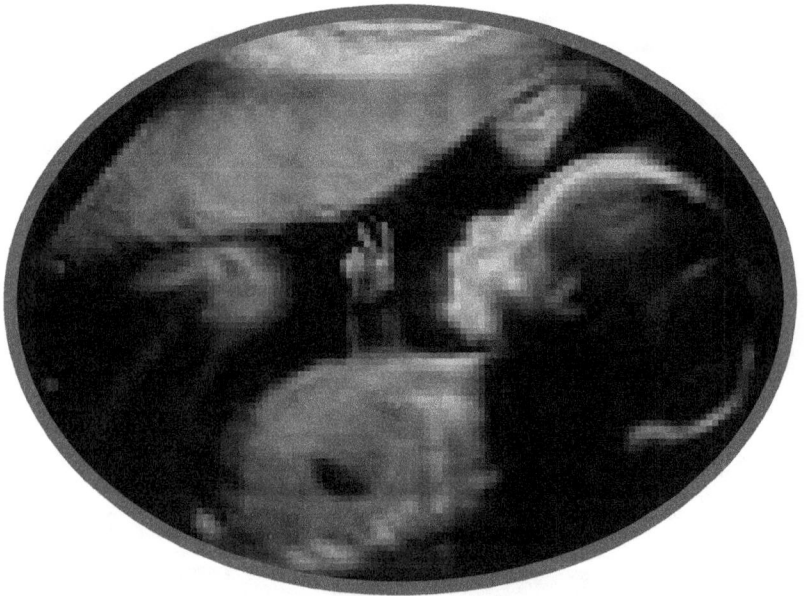

I remember thinking about my purpose before I even got here. Then I remembered a poem I wrote in the womb.

I guess it's safe to say that this is just the beginning.

TEACH THEM FETUS

If the price for freedom is death
then let the quest claim my life

what I'm saying is
we all must come to the point where we say
goodbye
and as we pass through time bloodlines
through the womb
you may find yourself in another room
somewhere in some other space
in the body of a baby
wearing someone else's face

can't quite figure out what just took place
I got dizzy living busy
I think murder was the case but I know I'm
supposed to be here
My purpose is to change the filter in the
atmosphere so that the energy of our Unity
will
devour fear

Yet the ability to connect through telepathy
will induce their fear
and I have yet to breathe the Air
message from the fetus
sounds like you really need this but there's
barcodes
names on a list
we've been here before?
trust me
it's just a myth
PA Buddha bless them with the gift
uplift and repair METAPHYSICS!!!!!!

I'm already here
this took place back in 65
I'm speaking right now feels good to be alive
feels good to be in death
transformation and subway stations ARE
what's coming next
so live to do your best
it is there you'll find the
secrets
of your success

*I remember the vibration Ahumdul-Allah, (all praises
due to Allah)*

*I remember Ahmad and the teachings of his quest, and I
thank him*
*I remember looping the vibe, creating a verbal chant
Ahumdul-Allah...Ahumdul-Allah...Ahumdul-Allah
over and over again*

*I remember a conversation I had with my oldest
daughter when she asked
"How do you know what's real and true?"
I said "Because I 'Will' it..."*

*I remember writing a poem to the flow and rhythm of
Ahumdul-Allah over and over again.
My conversation with Shayla has everything to do with
the lesson in this poem.*

That's my Shay.

AHUMDUL-ALLAH...AHUMDUL-ALLAH

Why not say that?
Why not speak that?
Why not believe in that!?!

Will to be one with the illumination of the
son
This is how life's won

Why wouldn't you say what you do?
You know I'm talking to you
You know I'm telling the truth

Will to be one with the positive expression
and don't turn your back on this lesson

Why are you hating?
Why don't you give a damn when I'm trying
to save the babies?

Will to be one with the love of the inner
Kingdom
G-Mill sent to free them
So don't be dumb
Pull your thumbs out your mouth
'Cause they building extra coffins in the
South

One way out
Mind over matter no doubt

This is what I'm talking bout

Will to be one with
Nebadon – "The local universe"

Where you really come from

Why not claim that?
Unlimited
Power
Let's bring peace back
Because we're under attack
Now let me get you where I'm at

Because The G-Mill kicks facts
Now watch The G-Mill kick back

Because you know I love you all
and to all ya'll believe that...

Will to be one
With the un-dead and watch me break
through
With this breaking news...breaking bread
Allah gives back
It's the only way of life
Now everybody say that

<u>WHEN I TALK</u>
(*this whole piece is sung*)

When I talk I just want you to listen

when I talk I just need you to listen

I'll send thoughts until you catch a vision

when I talk now you see how I get in

Into you I bring truth on a rhythm

disconnect the death style of a system

I transmit awareness through my passion

self control as you know starts by fasting

it's a goal to reach life everlasting

from a scroll it's the words that I'm casting

but my soul's feeling cold 'cause we're

clashing

it's the cash that you crave

no more freedom

now we live in this cave without freedom

junkie zombies all around me when I see them

and they act like they don't even need Him

too puffed up and too proud to get wisdom

can't believe you won't receive 'cause their too numb

can't let go of that old style they call fun

I was bought with His blood just to face them

now I'm sold 'cause I know I can save them

through the Lord I have made my decision

through the Lord I am saved by salvation

through Allah I am life through creation

through Allah I will raise up this nation

through my words I go deep penetration

uplifted the spirit with vibration

and it feels so good sensation

and it feels like I'mma bout to break them

Jesus always wins

that's the outcome

Ishadul Allah that's the outcome

Gary N. Miller Jr. "The G-Mill"

when I talk I just want you to have some

when I talk I just need you to have some

'cause this life's gonna roll off my tongue

and I speak peace in the land of my kingdom

and you're all invited to my season

where it's good and plentiful and pleasing

when I talk just let that be the reason

'cause my God, he can rise up an ocean

and my God put this thing in motion

with my god it's true devotion

with this poem it's the true love potion

so let us walk in the path of the Good Son

let us walk in the light of the bright sun

when I talk

let me talk

till I'm all done

WINNING SPIRIT

It's been said 'cause I heard this once before

it's that you and I are dead in a symbolic
metaphor

and I felt that way

number from reality

smothered from the anxieties of life

and that's like ice...water in my veins

or like a Slurpee froze my brain

I don't think like I claim

I'm insane from doing the same things

time and time again

and I can't help but complain

but it's strong and it's strange

I'm going through this pain

just to find out who I am

and then who are you?

You are like the planets and stars that hold down a soul

that I know on the level of flesh and bone

or you occupy the body of a guy

that I used to recognize

you see

I believe that we are all brothers in Christ

if you multiply your life by the number of branches

from each family tree

from each planted seed from 84 B.C.

to the year 2033

you are my brother

literally

and we should know this see

but the fields are many

where the ignorance is plenty

and the failure includes

for the seeds we plant are few

so as a planter

a farmer

or a fisherman

if I have to say it once then I'll say it over
again

walk in love

speak in love

you all know the meaning of Jesus

teaches God is Love

it's all about the story of us

'cause I believe in my heart that I've lead

and the message tastes like breakfast

'cause you and I

we just broke bread

you've been fed

'cause I meant what I said

every word that I used comes from Scripture
I've read

and I bled

so that all of you can hear it

maybe even catch the spirit

speak like this

bis-me Allah

so check your conscious and if you don't
wanna do it like this

and you don't wanna be righteous

and you wanna fool with anyone who might
just take a knife

and slice through your life

I get hyped with these lessons that I speak

they be priceless

and you like it

you like "man what's happening? I'm feeling
all Black again

when this dude be rappin' to me just like the African"

I'm not back again 'cause I never left

best believe what comes next

so repent and confess

I guess I wasted enough time

but keep in mind all the lines I express in my poetry rhymes

be blessed

stay in prayer and stay focused

let God be your style for the here and now

let the sound of my palms come to an end

with a simple

I love you all

and for all to say Amen

WINNING SPIRIT (PART 2)

Accepted – how do you top that?

How do you bring that face slap that cracked jaws?

that had all of you saying "awww, what did he say?"

knowing what you heard was real word

I served it to you in truth so pay attention and listen

while I smack you with this mood

'cause this crowd's in my town

in my sound

in my lounge

yes, yes, ya'll

you knows I get down

the holy spirit spins the flow off of my crown

so get in where you fit in and I mean that

right now

'cause I'm going to get crude with it

I mean downright rude with it

my mission in life is to keep you from losing it

so get to it

if I tell you that we're slipping

'cause when salt loses its flavor it never gets it back again

when I pour the Word of the Lord into the pit of your core

try not to mix it with too much beer and liquor

you feeling me?

claiming that you hearing me

making me fuss 'cause you really not receiving me

I trust you enough to give it up

but these bodies that we rock

don't even belong to us

'cause we mistreat it

when we smoke it

then we freak it

then we sneak it in the shadows

just to numb it 'cause we hate it

'cause the devil made us do it

so you'll dress it like a sadist

'cause you wanna feel nice but if you knew
why He died

you might not feel so nice

I know in my heart that I'm not teaching
nice

I know in my heart you might get hurt
tonight

but I need you to know

it hurts me deep inside but you know that I
know that

that ass is mine

so let's fall back for a minute and recheck

the signs

'cause I might not be talking to you

some of ya'll got your stuff together

I'm talking to the demon that thinks he's clever

I'm talking to the semen seeking surrogate mothers

I'm talking to them real slick

sharp mu-fuckers

but I'm talking in truth, 'cause I wanna make it better

so please forgive me for my language 'cause I need to get it together

but-the message that I'm sending stands stronger than ever

serve the Lord God only and He'll stay with you forever

these are the Words of Life and I wanna save your life

you guys believe me right?

you know I'm here out of fear and I'm
bringing you my best

I'm more than sincere for what my God can
do

so do this for me

pray

so that you can have a breakthrough

then you can have some cake too

and the blessings that He brings will simply
make you

accepted

in the eyes of Allah

EXPRESSION OF LOVE

This energy that I speak of (the love for a mother or loved one) is the same energy that my children feel for their Mother...it is life.

I remember hearing the statement "I Love You to Life". Powerful statement...author unknown.

I remember the feeling that came over me when my children entered the world...my children represent the endless possibilities that I leave behind...

Gary N. Miller Jr. "The G-Mill"

I LOVE YOU TO LIFE...

that just sounds right
makes me wanna say it twice
say it every day and night

I Love You to Life

uplift with all my might
saying things to change the sight
using thoughts to create time

I Love You to Life
I, like the sunlight
rays from my sun-rhymes
here comes the peace sign

I Love You to Life

Love you hard until there's nothing left
remember when I loved you to death?
wrong was my mind set

my condition was
I spoke from tradition
it was never my intention to mention
the mysteries of Auset
light and life over darkened death
that perception's from the left
let me bless you with some fresh breath

so I can tell you what's next

stand by for the Most High at the base of the
neck
GOD's mouth as you bow your heads
insert this information in the cerebral cortex
I flex, lessons in flight...no doubt about it
I'm-a shout it...

I Love You to Life

I remember my daughter Shelesse responded to my poem by writing one of her own...she gave me permission to use it.

I thank the Most High for my Lesse-Bear...

<u>LESSE'S POEM</u>
I love you to life
And now you're alive
I'm sorry for loving you to death
I'm glad you survived
I would say I'm here to hold you down
But that would be a lie
I'm here to uplift you
Right below the sky

I love you to life
Just so you can live
Live another day just so you can give
Give back the love you wanted dead
Give back the hate that has been spread
With that being said

I love you to life
Because I want to see you prevail
Listening to you in and exhale
That's real!!!
You're alive for a reason

so stop loving your loved ones to death

It's unbelievable how you can say something

and not know the true meaning
I say
I love you to life
to keep this world alive
and if you say it too
I don't see how the world could die!

(Crafted by Shelesse Miller...that was awesome...the apple doesn't fall far!)

<u>I LOVE YOU</u>

The greatest walk I ever took was the walk
that I took alone

I pounded concrete and turned that into
ivory stone

carved from the author of Life

Jesus Christ resurrected in me

means you're under siege

which means these minutes?

they belong to me

which means my words have authority

Yes, I too have returned from the dead

resurrected it's been tested

did you hear what I said?

I'll repeat it as needed

it's not the first time I entered minds
thorough

"The Jesus Teachings"

if you're searching like I'm seeking

you'll take heed to my sound

'cause I'm seeding you with verbs and nouns

words by the pound

into the depths of your ambitions

so let us make this our holy ground

let's surround it with some angels

they'll separate you to make sure that your

thoughts are true

because He died for you

I make it my business yet you're clueless to
my visit

I catch feelings from the ignorance

so I tap into the facts that bring back the
holy witness

I give it like it get it

I don't cut it

I just sift it then I word it so you hear it

God approves it

Spirits move it

then I spit it and it's music to the Lord

when I praise Him angels named Him

Jesus

He's us

new born fetus

free us

lead us to whatever is righteous

Jesus

lead us to whatever is admirable

Jesus lead us

to whatever is pure

that things you should think of with your

knees to the floor

and by the way Lord

can you open up some doors?

'cause the Spirit brought me through

and I wanna know

if this is what you want me to do

to bare my soul to you

I came to show and prove

bring you all this news

I come to watch you choose

so whether you win or lose try not to get
confused

I'm not just passing through

I come to pay my dues

because I Love You

DEDICATIONS

I dedicate this book to the Most High, the perfect energy that has placed me on the path of success, the true author of my life unfolding his way to peace, joy and abundance, I realized that the heavenly father set his agents at the precise time for the greatest prize, surrounding me with unconditional love and protection.

How strong my sister Dawn has been with her support in all of my journeys. Then there is Maia, subliminally taking my hand and guiding me to the greatness that I seek. My sisters are celestial, and I love them very much.

I thank God for the timing of it all, I thank all of my teachers who helped me overstand the perception of a man.

My wife Kenosha and what she brings has almost everything to do with me. Speak life into your wife...the connection can be epic...the reflection is the ticket.

I thank Ahmad for the lessons of vibrations, those keys

mean everything to me and because the Most High continues to place his disciples by my side. I thank him for Thomas, .he is the Kwoteman and his plans include me. I thank the Most High for the bright spots passing by and for those who kept my head above muddy waters. Respect for the nest is what the Most High ordered. My aunts Marty and Sandy, and my feisty little Nanny. I thank the mentor Adrian Rob for the pride and the jobs. I thank the angels from the other side, Ma Jo, Nana and aunt Di. I thank the recent energies that have been good to me...like Athena, Lee, Bonnie and Lillie.

I thank the energy of the past that would not let me fall. I thank you Joey, Marlon and Uncle Ronnie. I thank you all.

I thank the Most High for the poetry ride, the spoken word community that has adopted me...teaching the meaning of unity. I thank you Carla, Soul Cry, Tiger, Shane, Dustin, Chris, Nathaniel, Shaashawn, Glory, Major, Jubair, all of my poetry friends. Please forgive me if you weren't mentioned, you know I honor all specific moments.

I thank Andrea and T.L. for their expertise and positive energy in bringing life to this project.

Finally the Greatest part of me...my father who was dead on when he planted his seeds, raising me in the best way he saw fit...Yes, Dad you are my King, and I will always know this.

Gary N. Miller Jr. "The G-Mill"

I thank Shayla, Shelesse, and my oldest son Gary for

believing in my dreams...and for that I will through the Most High, restore a great Kingdom for you all, that you may be proud to claim me as your father. For my son Cameron, although we missed the opportunity to bond, I

want you here to share and connect to the royalty that is me. I love you all so much...

To think that all of this comes from the womb of my Mom...thank you Mom, I Love You.

God knows how much I appreciate the timing of it all.

Glossary

Ahumdul-Allah – all praises due to Allah

A-mon - (Amen – be it so)

Auset – the true archetype of a goddess (Isis), ideal mother and wife of nature and magic

Bis me Allah – with the assistance of Allah

Bismeillaahir Rahmaaneir Raheim – the beginning of the "Al Fatiha" which is an Islamic prayer

Darma – when you allow God to make all of your decisions (Deepak Chopra)

Dikahru-Allah – in remembrance of Allah

Djed – the spine

Elo – another name for the Most High

Elohim – children of the Most High

E-Mon – with unshakeable faith

Nebadon – the name of the local universe in which the Earth dwells or belongs.

Ramadan – 9th month of the Islamic calendar, followers fast for inner reflection and devotion to God

Sadhu – never ceases to exist, lasts forever

Se-kum – the life force (Kemetic definition)

Universal Law – a natural law that cannot be changed by man (ex: gravity)

Yashua-Bin-Joseph – the Son of Mary and Joseph (another name for Jesus)

Yahweh – the vibration that brings the will to be

Yahweh El-Elyon – the Universal Father (aka the Most High Power)

Yireh – the creative energy that wills that which you ask for into existence

(Definitions from "The Ancient Mysteries of Melchizedek" (Melchizedek Y. Lewis), The Holy Quran, and The King James version of the Bible)

About the Author

Gary N. Miller, Jr. aka The G-Mill is a Harrisburg, PA native. He is a loving father, son, husband and friend.

He feels that life is about your "calling". He fell right into this poetry thing that is his calling and that "was meant to be." All of the things he has done in his past have prepared him for this poetic journey and he is thankful for the timing of it all.

"Poetry Rising" is the first of many collections to come.

The G-Mill can be followed on Twitter: @gmillpoet

and on Facebook:

https://www.facebook.com/TheGMill

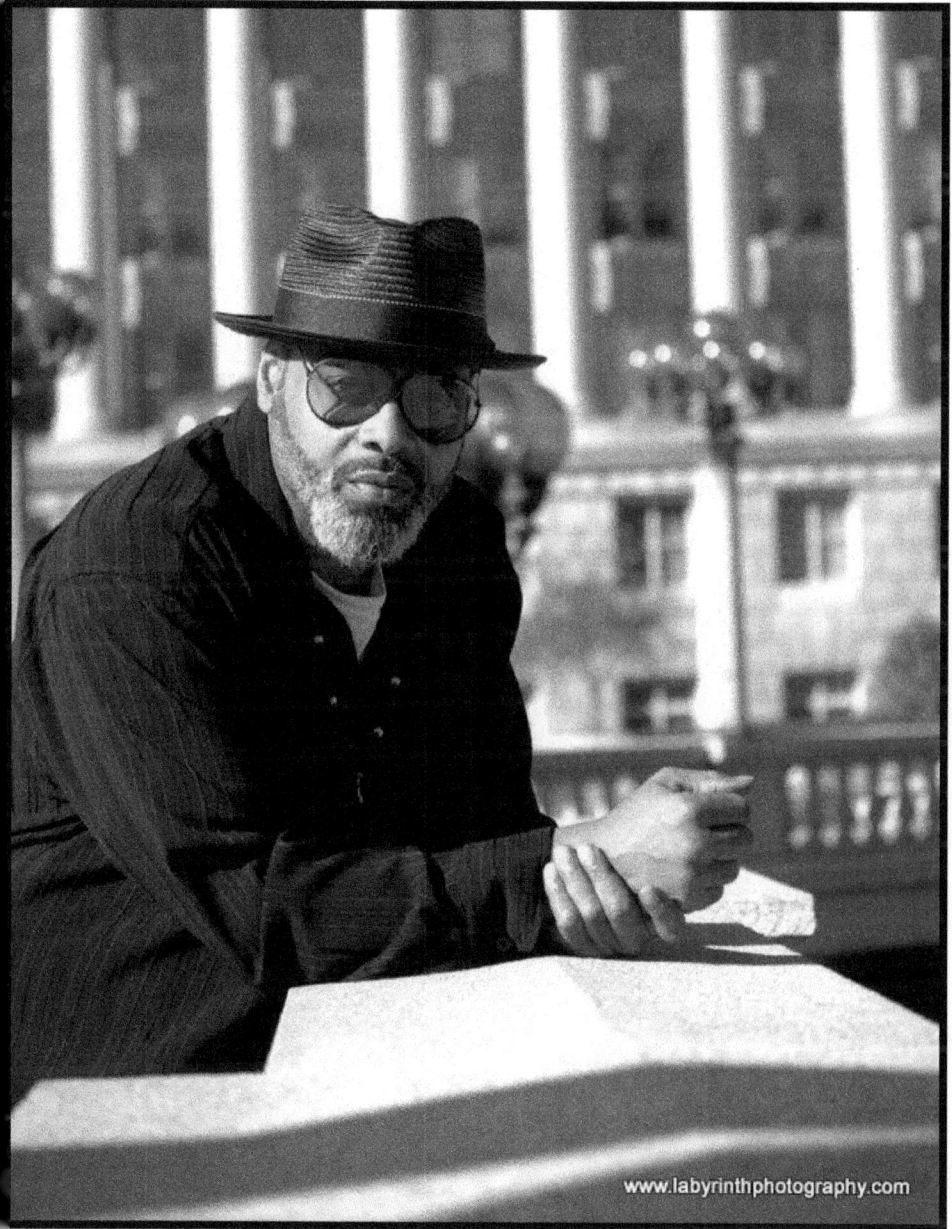

www.labyrinthphotography.com

Gary N. Miller Jr. "The G-Mill"

Other Publications by Waid Books

Love and Other Misunderstandings- T.L. Waid

Something Sensual- T.L. Waid

Recipes Made With P-Love's Smokin' Rub- Kevin "Pete" Groom

Themes and Dreams- Andrea R. Cunningham

Tales From The Concrete Jungle- Michael Allen

The Woman Within- Stormy Scott

www.waidbooks.com

https://www.facebook.com/WaidBooks

twitter @waidbooks

Poetry Rising

www.ingramcontent.com/pod-product-compliance
Lightning Source LLC
Chambersburg PA
CBHW060807050426
42449CB00008B/1585